CU00842097

Magical Oil Recipes

Essential Oil Blends by Intent

LADY GIANNE

Copyright © 2011 by Lady Gianne
All rights reserved. No part of this publication may be
reproduced, distributed, or transmitted in any form or by
any means, including photocopying, recording, or other
electronic or mechanical methods, without the prior
written permission of the publisher, except in the case of
brief quotations embodied in critical reviews and certain
other noncommercial uses permitted by copyright law.
First Printing, 2011
Revised 2013

Anointing Oils

Astrological Oils

Blessing Oils

Chakra Oils

Elemental Oils

Health and Healing Oils

Love Oils

Personal Power Oils

Planetary Oils

Protection Oils

Psychic Energy Oils

Sabbat Oils

Sexual Oils

Success Oils

Wealth Oils

Uses of Magical Oil

Magical oil is very useful to practitioners of all types of magic. It can be used:

- To anoint candles for candle burning rituals.
- To anoint, consecrate, or bless ritual objects.
- To wear to increase certain powers or talents you would like to enhance, with an added bonus of having a pleasing scent.
- As a substitute for burning incense to experience a particular scent if you are in a place where incense is frowned upon.

Combining Your Own Oil

Many witches prefer to create their own magical oils. By creating the oil blend personally, their own power and intent will be transferred to the blend, which cannot happen when buying premade blends. It can also be more cost efficient to create your own blends.

All of the blends in this book assume a carrier oil plus essential oils. Recipes are based on essential oil, not synthetic. While synthetic oil is generally much cheaper than essential oil and might smell similar, synthetic does not hold any magical properties as it is missing the root and essence of the plant.

Please be ware some essential oils can be toxic, harmful to skin, harmful to ingest, or cause allergic reactions in some people. Always use caution and good judgment. If you are creating a blend that will be worn on the skin or added to a bath, it needs to be tested before you get it all over yourself or someone else.

An easy way to test is to dab a small amount of the oil on your arm or elbow, and wait a few hours. If nothing happens, you probably aren't allergic.

Always, if you are unsure whether or not an essential oil can be ingested, don't ingest it or else do good research beforehand. With a good bit of common sense everyone can practice magic safely.

Carrier Oils

Carrier oil is the base oil which you start with. Carrier oils are as follows: almond, olive, safflower, and sunflower. You can use any carrier oil you prefer. Olive oil is perhaps the cheapest one on the list, depending on the type and brand. It is also probably the least attractive smelling to many people.

When selecting carrier oil, keep in mind the purpose to which you will use your magical oil blend. If you are creating a blend to anoint candles or other objects, olive oil is probable fine and is cost efficient. If you are creating an oil rub for your body, you might want to select almond oil, something many people like on their skin.

Oil Storage

It is very important to understand how to store magical oils properly. Basic essential oils tend to be expensive. Once you have created a magical oil blend suited to your specific purpose, it is in your best interest to store it properly, saving you time and money in the long run.

When you are ready to create your magical oil blend, assemble your tools. All tools, and especially the bottles that will be used for storage, should be boiled for at least ten minutes before use. This will ensure that there isn't dirt or bacteria on anything that could contaminate your supply.

You will need to store your oil in glass bottles. Never store oil in a plastic bottle, even though plastic is much cheaper. Using a glass bottle will ensure you are able to utilize your magical oil blend as long as possible, while using plastic will simply hasten its going bad.

Your glass bottle should also be made of colored glass, as this will help block out light. Green or brown are good colors for storing magical oil. Some people will prefer to store each magical oil blend in a glass bottle with a color that corresponds to its purpose.

This is a good idea if you can manage to locate small glass bottles in a variety of colors. Once your blend is complete, it should be marked by its name and date, and then stored in a cool, dark place. Oils will generally last for six months.

Oil Correspondence

Acacia: holy, meditation, psychic power, purification

Almond: base oil

Allspice: strengthening, vitality

Bay: attraction, money, purification

Benzoin: cleansing, purification, strengthening

Bergamot: financial gain, protection

Black Pepper: courage, strength, protection, general power increase

Chamomile: peace, mediation, rest

Camphor: purification, basic power

Cardamom: love, sexuality, romance

Carnation: love, power, healing

Cedar: spirituality, protection, peace

Cinnamon: psychic ability increase, wealth attraction, good luck

Clove: courage, protection

Coriander: healing

Cypress: calmness, consecration, protection,

Eucalyptus: healing, purification

Frankincense: mediation, blessings

Geranium: promotes calm, stimulant, healing

Ginger: sexuality, financial gain

Grapefruit: purification, popularity

Jasmine: love, sexuality, romance, marriage

Juniper: luck, protection

Lavender: peace, love, emotional healing

Lilac: harmony, psychic ability, improve memory, longevity

Lemon: healing, purification, protection

Lemongrass: soothing, calming

Lime: protection, faith

Magnolia: love, mediation

Musk: courage, fertility, sexuality

Myrrh: protection, strength, peace of mind

Orange: relaxation, relationships

Patchouli: aphrodisiac, communication

Peppermint: excitement, stimulant, mental powers, headache relief
Pine: mental clarity, cleanse negativity

Rose: love, passion, romance, fertility

Rosemary: emotional healing, calming

Sandalwood: promotes dreaming, release of emotions, mental power

Sweet Pea: loyalty, affection

Tangerine: calming, relieves stress

Vanilla: happiness, good fortune

Vetivert: protection

Violet: love, marriage

Wisteria: good fortune, prosperity

Ylang ylang: peace, sex, love

Basic Oil Recipe

For each magical oil blend, begin with 1/8 cup of carrier oil. Add the drops of essential oil to the carrier oil, per the recipe. To combine, swish or swirl the oil around, do not stir. Your oil is complete.

If you only need a very small amount of the blend you are making, you can start with less than 1/8 cup of carrier oil, simply reduce the drops by a corresponding amount.

Altar Oil

10 drops rose oil
10 drops walnut oil
Acorn if you are male, rosebud if you are female

Altar Oil II

10 drops myrrh
10 drops cedar

Altar Oil III

5 drops frankincense
5 drops myrrh
1 drop cedar

Anointing Oil

4 drops myrrh
3 drops cinnamon

Anointing Oil II

3 drops lime
3 drops lemon
3 drops orange

Anointing Oil III

4 drops lily of the valley
2 drops honeysuckle
1 drop violet
1 drop lemon

Initiation Oil

3 drop bay
3 drops musk
1 drop myrrh

Aquarius Oil

4 drops acacia
2 drop cypress
1 drop lavender

Aries Oil

4 drops carnation
1 drop cedar
1 drop cinnamon

Cancer Oil

4 drops gardenia
2 drops lemon
1 drop violet

Capricorn Oil

3 drops chamomile
2 drops vanilla
1 drops lemon

Gemini Oil

3 drops bergamot
1 drop clover
1 drop lavender
1 drop lilac

Leo Oil

3 drops cinnamon
2 drops frankincense
1 drop musk

Libra Oil

4 drops apple
4 drops cat nip
1 drop magnolia
1 drop sweet pea

Pisces Oil

3 drops basil
3 drops lemon

Sagittarius Oil

3 drops borage oil
4 drops saffron oil
1 drop sage oil

Scorpio Oil

3 drops basil
2 drops clove
1 drop ylang ylang

Taurus Oil

3 drop peppermint
1 drop thyme
1 drops catnip

Virgo Oil

7 drops peppermint oil

Blessing Oil

4 drops myrrh
4 drops cedar
Amber

Goddess Oil

5 drops rose
1 drop jasmine
1 drop lemon
1 drop ambergris or cypress

Mother Goddess Oil

4 drops myrrh
3 drops cypress
2 drops rose
1 drop ylang ylang

Basic Chakra Oil

3 drops lemon
3 drops orange
3 drops lavender
3 drops myrrh
3 drops clove

1st (Root) Chakra Oil

3 drops cinnamon
3 drops musk

2nd (Spine) Chakra Oil

3 drops orange
3 drops sandalwood

3rd (Solar Plexus) Chakra Oil

3 drops frankincense
3 drops honeysuckle
3 drops lemon

4th (Heart) Chakra Oil

3 drops ylang ylang
3 drops eucalyptus
3 drops violet
3 drops vanilla

5th (Throat) Chakra Oil

2 drops cedar
2 drops clove
2 drops rosemary

6th (Third Eye) Chakra Oil

4 drops carnation
4 drops rosemary
4 drops lavender

7th (Crown) Chakra Oil

1 drop myrrh
1 drop lotus
1 drop frankincense
1 drop camphor
1 drop clove

Elemental Air Oil
Carrier oil specific: almond

3 drops lavender
3 drops sage
3 drops bergamot

Elemental Air Oil II

6 drops lavender
4 drops lemongrass
1 drop peppermint

Elemental Earth Oil

9 drops honey
7 drops magnolia
3 drops pine
1 drop patchouli

Elemental Earth Oil II

3 drops magnolia
3 drops vetivert
1 drop primrose

Elemental Fire Oil

11 drops orange
9 drops nutmeg
3 drops cinnamon
1 drop clove

Elemental Fire Oil II

3 drops cedar
2 drops rosemary
2 drops orange

Elemental Spirit Oil

7 drops sandalwood
7 drops violet
3 drops crocus
3 drops gardenia

Elemental Water Oil

9 drops sweet pea
7 drops camellia
5 drops jasmine
3 drops lotus

Fast Healing Oil

3 drops rosemary
2 drops juniper
1 drop sandalwood

Healing Oil

4 drops rosemary
3 drops juniper
2 drops sandalwood

Healing Oil II

4 drops rosemary
3 drops lavender
2 drops sandalwood

Healing Oil III

3 drops chamomile
2 drops camphor
1 drop pine

Health Oil

3 drops eucalyptus
3 drops orange
3 drops lemon

Affection Oil

3 drops gardenia
1 drop jasmine
1 drop musk

Come to me Oil

3 drops sandalwood
3 drops rose
1 drop cinnamon

Come to me Oil II

5 drops carnation
3 drops magnolia

Love Attraction Oil

4 drops musk
3 drops cassia
2 drops sandalwood
1 drop myrrh

Love Attraction Oil II

4 drops rose
4 drops cinnamon
2 drops clove

Love Attraction Oil III

9 drops vanilla
1 drops cinnamon
1 drops peppermint

Love Oil
Carrier oil specific: almond oil

7 drops acacia
6 drops ylang ylang
3 drops jasmine
1 drop lilac
1 drop lemon

Love Oil II

7 drops rose
5 drops ylang ylang
3 drops lavender
1 drop ginger

Calming Oil

5 drops benzoin
4 drops vanilla
1 drop cinnamon

Courage Oil

2 drops ylang ylang
1 drop camphor
1 drop clove

Energy Oil

4 drops orange
4 drops lime
3 drops cardamom

Energy Oil II

3 drops ginger
2 drops black pepper
1 drop wisteria

Grace Oil

1 drop patchouli
1 drop juniper
1 drop pine
1 drop cedar

Happiness Oil

7 drops lemon
7 drops lavender
2 drops lime

Luck Oil

3 drops mimosa
3 drops carnation
3 drops patchouli

Peace Oil

9 drops catnip
1 drop clove

Peace Oil II

3 drops wisteria
3 drops lilac
1 drop cedar
1 drop cypress

Powerful Oil

2 drops patchouli
2 drops ginger
1 drop black pepper
1 drop peppermint

Full Moon Oil

3 drops lemon
2 drops sandalwood
1 drop rose

Jupiter Oil

1 drop clove
1 drop cardamom
1 drop black pepper

Lunar Oil

3 drops spearmint
2 drops eucalyptus
1 drop lemon
1 drop cypress

Lunar Oil II

4 drops sandalwood
2 drops camphor
1 drop lemon

Lunar Oil III

1 drop jasmine
1 drop sandalwood

Mars Oil

5 drops orange
5 drops apple
1 drops vanilla

Mercury Oil

3 drops lavender
3 drops eucalyptus
1 drop peppermint

Saturn Oil

5 drops comfrey

Solar Oil

4 drops honey
4 drops apple
Amber

Solar Oil II

15 drops lemon
1 drop lime
Gold

Venus Oil

4 drops peppermint
3 drops raspberry
1 drop rose

Banishing Oil

1 drop carnation
1 drop bay
1 drop clove

Cleanse Negativity Oil

3 drops orange
2 drops lemongrass
2 drops lemon
2 drops lime

Defense Oil

3 drops myrrh
2 drops cypress
1 drop patchouli
Mint leaf

Protection Oil

4 drops basil
3 drops pine
2 drops oregano
1 drop vetivert

Protection Oil II

9 drops bay
7 drops chamomile
1 drop pine
1 drop black pepper

Protection Oil III

3 drops frankincense
3 drops sandalwood
Amber

Purification Oil

3 drops musk
3 drops myrrh
1 drop frankincense

Purification Oil II

4 drops lilac
4 drops lemongrass
1 drop lemon
1 drop lime

Purification Oil III

4 drops benzoin
3 drops bergamot
1 drop camphor

Astral Travel Oil

2 drops frankincense
2 drops myrrh
2 drops cypress
2 drops jasmine

Astral Travel Oil II

4 drops grapefruit
2 drops patchouli
1 drop tangerine

Divination Oil

5 drops vetivert
5 drops musk
3 drops ambergris
3 drops violet
1 drop lilac

Powerful Dream Oil

5 drops sandalwood
2 drops ylang ylang
2 drops cinnamon

Powerful Speech Oil

4 drops ylang ylang
2 drops lavender
1 drop rose

Psychic Oil

4 drops lemongrass
3 drops bay
1 drop nutmeg

Psychic Oil II

7 drops cedar
3 drops myrrh
3 drops violet
3 drops musk
1 drop ambergris

Quickening Oil

5 drops mimosa
1 drop hyacinth
1 drop sandalwood
1 drop cinnamon

Spiritual Oil

6 drops sandalwood
4 drops cedar
1 drop frankincense

Basic Sabbat Oil

2 drops apple
2 drops juniper
1 drop cypress
1 drop sage

Beltane Oil

Carrier oil specific: almond

3 drops apple
3 drops calendula
3 drops frankincense
3 drops lilac

Imbolc Oil

2 drops basil
2 drops bay
3 drops cinnamon
1 drop rosemary

Lammas Oil

5 drops apple
5 drops blackberry
1 drop frankincense

Mabon Sabbat Oil

Carrier oil specific: almond

9 drops walnut
9 drops marigold
Quartz crystal

Midsummer Sabbat Oil

10 drops violet
10 drops elder
5 drops lavender
5 drops patchouli

Midsummer Sabbat Oil II

3 drops hazelnut
3 drops elder
3 drops lavender
3 drops rosemary

Ostara Oil

1 drop iris
1 drop jasmine
1 drop lavender
1 drop rose

Samhain Oil

3 drops pine
3 drops frankincense
2 drops lavender

Yule Sabbat Oil

3 drops pine
3 drops frankincense
3 drops patchouli
1 drop lavender

Fertility Oil

4 drops lilac
2 drops violet
2 drops honeysuckle
1 drop lemon

Sexual Energy Oil

2 drops bay
2 drops cedar
1 drop lavender
1 drop black pepper

Success Oil

3 drops heliotrope
2 drops lavender
1 drop patchouli

Success Oil II

2 drops myrrh
2 drops vetivert
2 drops lavender

Business Success Oil

5 drops bay
2 drops allspice
1 drop juniper
1 drop pine

Business Success Oil II

4 drops basil
4 drops ginger
1 drop spearmint

Fast Money Oil

6 drops bergamot
5 drops lemon
4 drops lime
3 drops geranium

Fast Money Oil II

10 drops patchouli

Money Attraction Oil

3 drops patchouli
3 drops bay
3 drops pine

Money Attraction Oil II

7 drops patchouli
6 drops cedar
5 drops vetivert
1 drop ginger

Retain Wealth Oil

3 drops cinnamon
2 drops gardenia
1 drop bay

Unexpected Wealth Attraction Oil

10 drops lily of the valley
5 drops rose
5 drops sandalwood
3 drops mimosa
3 drops cinnamon

Wealth Attraction Oil

5 drops peppermint
5 drops lemon

Also by Lady Gianne

CPSIA information can be obtained
at www.ICGtesting.com
Printed in the USA
LVOW12s1602100418
572940LV00001B/193/P